# Ocean Animals

# Crabs

by Derek Zobel

BELLWETHER MEDIA
MINNEAPOLIS, MN

**Blastoff! Beginners** are developed by literacy experts and educators to meet the needs of early readers. These engaging informational texts support young children as they begin reading about their world. Through simple language and high frequency words paired with crisp, colorful photos, Blastoff! Beginners launch young readers into the universe of independent reading.

Blastoff! Universe

Reading Level — Grade K

Grades 1-3

Grade 4

## Sight Words in This Book 🔍

| | | | | |
|---|---|---|---|---|
| a | did | is | there | who |
| and | eat | many | they | |
| are | from | new | this | |
| be | have | she | to | |
| big | her | the | too | |
| can | in | them | water | |

This edition first published in 2021 by Bellwether Media, Inc.

No part of this publication may be reproduced in whole or in part without written permission of the publisher. For information regarding permission, write to Bellwether Media, Inc., Attention: Permissions Department, 6012 Blue Circle Drive, Minnetonka, MN 55343.

Library of Congress Cataloging-in-Publication Data

Names: Zobel, Derek, 1983- author.
Title: Crabs / by Derek Zobel.
Description: Minneapolis, MN : Bellwether Media, 2021. | Series: Blastoff! beginners: ocean animals | Includes bibliographical references and index. | Audience: Ages PreK-2 | Audience: Grades K-1
Identifiers: LCCN 2020031977 (print) | LCCN 2020031978 (ebook) | ISBN 9781644873717 (library binding) | ISBN 9781648340727 (ebook)
Subjects: LCSH: Crabs--Juvenile literature.
Classification: LCC QL444.M33 Z63 2021 (print) | LCC QL444.M33 (ebook) | DDC 595.3/86--dc23
LC record available at https://lccn.loc.gov/2020031977
LC ebook record available at https://lccn.loc.gov/2020031978

Editor: Amy McDonald    Designer: Andrea Schneider

Printed in the United States of America, North Mankato, MN.

# Table of Contents

# Crabs!

Who is in
the sand?
A crab!

Crabs are
flat animals.
They live in
sand or water.

Crabs can be
big or small.
There are
many kinds.

blue

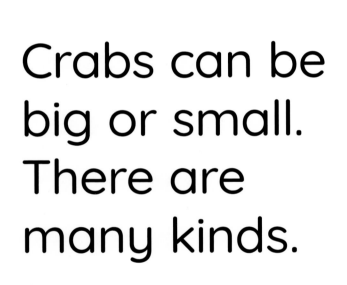

# Body Parts

Crabs have shells.
The shells
**protect** them.

shell

Crabs have
ten legs.
They **scuttle**
from side to side.

legs

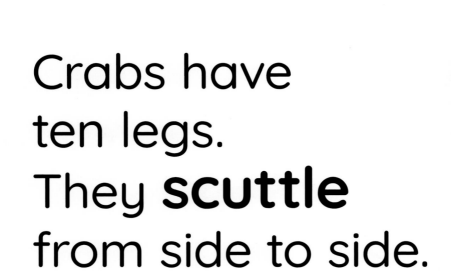

scuttle

Crabs have claws.
They grab food.

claw

food

# Growing Up

Crabs eat fish and clams. They eat plants, too.

**plants**

fish

This crab grew big. Her shell is too small. She needs to **molt**.

This crab did molt.
A new shell grows!

new shell

molted shell

# Crab Facts

## Crab Parts

shell

legs

claws

## Crab Food

fish

clams

small plants

# Glossary

**molt**

to shed skin
or a shell away

**protect**

to keep safe

**scuttle**

to walk with short,
fast steps

# To Learn More

## ON THE WEB

## FACTSURFER

Factsurfer.com gives you a safe, fun way to find more information.

1. Go to www.factsurfer.com.

2. Enter "crabs" into the search box and click 🔍.

3. Select your book cover to see a list of related content.

# Index

The images in this book are reproduced through the courtesy of: Yutthasart Yanakornsiri, front cover; Fahroni, p. 3; RainervonBrandis, pp. 4, 23 (scuttle); imacoconut, pp. 4-5; tracielouise, pp. 6-7; Tiger Images, pp. 8 (blue), 22 (parts); WagnerLessa, pp. 8-9; Nastya Dubrovina, p. 9 (Japanese spider); MYN/ Jerry Monkman/ NaturePL/ SuperStock, p. 9 (Jonah); Sean Lema, p. 10; Micael Zeigler, pp. 10-11; GlobalP, p. 12; Acsanova, pp. 12-13; Alexander Sviridov, p. 14; Jack Deagon, pp. 14-15; Jiang Hongyan, p. 16 (plant); Purisimo, pp. 16-17; Noah Zeitlin, pp. 18-19; Henry William Fu, pp. 20, 23 (molt); Jay Fleming/ Getty Images, pp. 20-21; evantravels, p. 22 (fish); Ingrid Maasik, pp. 22 (clams); Davdeka, p. 22 (small plants); fizkes, p. 23 (protect).